USING
MATHS
SOLVE A CRIME

by Wendy Clemson, David Clemson,
Kev Pritchard and Dr. Allison Jones

ticktock

USING
MATHS
SOLVE A CRIME

Copyright © ticktock Entertainment Ltd 2004

First published in Great Britain in 2004 by ticktock Media Ltd.,
Unit 2, Orchard Business Centre, North Farm Road, Tunbridge Wells, Kent, TN2 3XF

ISBN 1 86007 548 7 pbk
ISBN 1 86007 554 1 hbk
Printed in China

With thanks to our consultants: Jenni Back and Liz Pumfrey from the NRICH Project,
Cambridge University and Debra Voege.
With special thanks to Lorna Cowan.

WENDY CLEMSON

Wendy is experienced in working with and for children, and has been writing full-time since 1989. Her publications, which now exceed one hundred, have been written for children and sometimes their parents and teachers. In her many maths books, the aim is always to present the reader with challenges that are fun to do.

DAVID CLEMSON

David has wide-ranging experience as a writer and educationalist. His publications list is prodigious. In collaboration with Wendy, David has worked on many maths books for children. He is fascinated by maths and logic puzzles and is keen for the reader to enjoy them too.

KEV PRITCHARD

Kev is an experienced Scenes of Crime Officer (SOCO) with many years experience of examining crime scenes of every type. He is now a senior lecturer in the *Department of Forensic and Investigative Science* at the University of Central Lancashire, where he trains the SOCOs, detectives and forensic scientists of the future.

DR. ALLISON JONES

Allison is a forensic scientist. Her past experience includes the development of car paint analysis and the analysis of sunscreens. Allison is now a senior lecturer in the *Department of Forensic and Investigative Science* at the University of Central Lancashire, where she teaches the use of analytical techniques in forensic science and the practices involved in the handling and analysis of forensic evidence.

CONTENTS

HOW TO USE THIS BOOK   4-5

999 – THERE HAS BEEN A BURGLARY!   6-7

THE CRIME SCENE   8-9

EXAMINING THE CRIME SCENE   10-11

RECOVERING EVIDENCE   12-13

WITNESS STATEMENTS   14-15

INTERVIEWING SUSPECTS   16-17

ANALYSING CLUES: THE FOOTPRINTS   18-19

ANALYSING CLUES: BLOOD AND HAIR   20-21

ANALYSING CLUES: FINGERPRINTS   22-23

TIME TO CONFRONT YOUR SUSPECT   24-25

FINDING THE STOLEN GOODS   26-27

TIPS FOR MATHS SUCCESS   28-29

ANSWERS   30-31

GLOSSARY OF DETECTIVE WORDS
and MATHS GLOSSARY   32

NUMERACY WORK COVERED IN THIS BOOK:

CALCULATIONS:
Throughout this book there are opportunities to practise **addition**, **subtraction**, **multiplication** and **division** using both mental calculation strategies and pencil and paper methods.

NUMBERS AND THE NUMBER SYSTEM:
- COMPARING NUMBERS: pg. 14
- DECIMALS: pg. 19
- ESTIMATING: pg. 12
- FRACTIONS: pg. 19

SOLVING 'REAL LIFE' PROBLEMS:
- CODES: pg. 24
- MEASURES: pgs. 10, 14
- MONEY: pg. 6
- TIME: pgs. 10, 16

HANDLING DATA:
- BAR CHARTS: pg. 18
- CARROLL DIAGRAMS: pg. 20
- TALLY CHARTS: pg. 21
- USING TABLES/CHARTS/DIAGRAMS: pgs. 8, 9, 10, 11, 12, 14, 15, 22

MEASURES:
- AREA: pg. 23
- RELATIONSHIPS BETWEEN UNITS OF MEASUREMENT: pg. 14
- TIME (reading from analogue clocks): pg. 17
- USING METRIC/IMPERIAL MEASUREMENTS: pgs. 10, 14, 18
- VOCABULARY (time): pg. 16

SHAPE AND SPACE:
- 2-D SHAPES: pgs. 6, 27
- COMPASS DIRECTIONS: pg. 26
- GRID CO-ORDINATES: pg. 9
- REFLECTIVE SYMMETRY: pg. 27

Supports the maths work taught at Key Stage 2

HOW TO USE THIS BOOK

Maths is important in the lives of people everywhere. We use maths when we play a game, ride a bike, go shopping – in fact, all the time! Everyone needs to use maths at work. You may not realise it, but a detective would use maths to solve a crime! With this book you will get the chance to try lots of exciting maths activities using real life data and facts about the work of detectives and forensic scientists. Practise your maths and numeracy skills and experience the thrill of what it's really like to solve a crime.

This exciting maths book is very easy to use – check out what's inside!

Fun to read information about crime solving.

WITNESS STATEMENTS

Several good pieces of **evidence** have been found at the crime scene – the footprints, the broken glass with blood splashes, the single hair, the palm print and some **fingerprints**! It is not just physical evidence, such as fingerprints, that are collected at a crime scene. Detectives can also collect verbal (spoken) evidence, by taking **statements** from **witnesses**, **victims** and **suspects**. One of the millionaire's neighbours has given you some interesting information. The neighbour cannot walk very well, so she spends her days watching from her window. On the day of the burglary, she saw someone running from the mansion's back gate dressed in black and wearing a hat!

MATHS ACTIVITIES

Look for the
YELLOW CLIPBOARDS.
You will find real life maths activities and questions to try.

To answer some of the questions, you will need to collect data from a DATA BOX. Sometimes, you will need to collect facts and data from the text or from charts and diagrams.

Be prepared! You will need a pen or pencil and a notebook for your workings and answers.

DETECTIVE WORK

The person the neighbour saw was wearing white trainers and glasses and was taller than the mansion's gate. The gate is — *one hundred and sixty seven centimetres* high.

Everyone who lives or works at the mansion, or who was seen near the house on the day of the burglary, has been interviewed. The suspects were asked if they ever wear glasses, if they own a pair of white trainers and for their height.
Their answers have been put in the DATA BOX.
Use the data to answer these questions:

1) How many people never wear glasses?
2) Who does not own white trainers?
3) Which two suspects are the same height?
4) What is the difference in height between the tallest person and the shortest person?
5) Which of the suspects could the neighbour have seen running from the mansion's back gate?

(Don't forget to write the names of your suspects into your own notebook.)

(You will find a TIP to help you with these questions on page 28)

SOCO FACT

SOCOs are trained in a special interview technique called *cognitive interviewing*. They interview the victims of crimes, then use special 'E-Fit' computer software to produce a likeness of the **perpetrator's** face.

14

Fun to read facts about forensic science and the work of detectives.

If you see one of these boxes, there will be important data inside that will help you with the maths activities.

Feeling confident? Try these extra **CHALLENGE QUESTIONS.**

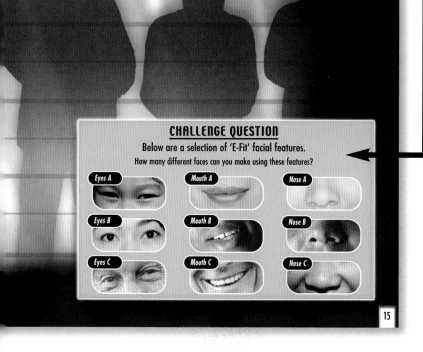

DATA BOX **TABLE OF SUSPECTS**

SUSPECT	SOMETIMES WEARS GLASSES	OWNS WHITE TRAINERS	HEIGHT
1. Delivery man	Yes	No	1 m 52 cm
2. Millionaire's secretary	Yes	Yes	1 ¾ metres
3. Man seen jogging nearby	No	Yes	2 m
4. The gardener	Yes	Yes	One metre and eighty centimetres
5. The chef	Yes	Yes	174 cm
6. The butler	Yes	Yes	He is not sure, but he is taller than the secretary.
7. The millionaire's maid	Yes	Yes	150 cm
8. Millionaire's personal trainer	Yes	Yes	1 metre 90 centimetres
9. The chauffeur	Yes	Yes	175 centimetres
10. The odd-job man	Yes	Yes	1720 mm

CHALLENGE QUESTION
Below are a selection of 'E-Fit' facial features.
How many different faces can you make using these features?

Eyes A   Mouth A   Nose A
Eyes B   Mouth B   Nose B
Eyes C   Mouth C   Nose C

15

IF YOU NEED HELP...

TIPS FOR MATHS SUCCESS
On pages 28 – 29 you will find lots of tips to help you with your maths work.

ANSWERS
Turn to pages 30 – 31 to check your answers.
(Try all the activities and questions before you take a look at the answers.)

GLOSSARY
On page 32 there is a glossary of detective words and a glossary of maths words. The glossary words appear **in bold** in the text.

999 – THERE HAS BEEN A BURGLARY!

There has been a burglary at the luxury mansion of a millionaire. The millionaire is away on his yacht, and one of his servants has just discovered the crime. The first police officer to arrive at the scene of a crime in response to a 999 call, is called the *First Officer Attending (FOA)*. The FOA secures the scene using police tape, this stops people walking about over the crime scene, destroying **evidence**. Next, the FOA calls for any assistance needed, for example, a detective and a **Scenes of Crime Officer (SOCO)** and an ambulance if someone is injured. Today, you are the detective on duty. Grab your notebook and pencil – it is time to get to work.

DETECTIVE WORK

The safe is empty! All that the thief has left behind are some bands from the bundles of bank notes and some of the empty boxes where the millionaire's jewels were kept.

1) In the DATA BOX you will see the bands that came off the missing money. How much was stolen?

Look at the jewel boxes in the DATA BOX.
The missing gems have left holes in the boxes.
The holes have made five shapes.
For example, there is a square in the sapphires box.
2) Which of the boxes are these shapes in?
- a) **Equilateral triangle**   b) **Isoceles triangle**
- c) **Hexagon**   d) **Octagon**

Here are the values given to each of the gemstones:
- Diamond £100 • Sapphire £85 • Ruby £65

3) What is the value of the stolen gems in each of the jewel boxes:
Box A) Sapphires?
Box B) Rubies?
Box C) Diamonds?

(You will find TIPS to help you with these questions on page 28)

POLICE WORK FACT

The FOA starts off the police investigation. On arrival at the scene, the FOA thinks through some important questions. What has happened here? What evidence has been left behind? Is there any evidence that needs protection from the weather? Where is the **perpetrator** now?

CRIME SCENE FACT

Depending on the type of crime, different personnel will be called to a crime scene. These can include SOCOs and **forensic scientists**, police dog handlers and their dogs (when searching for drugs) and fire and explosives officers for arson (fire) investigations.

WHAT HAS BEEN STOLEN FROM THE SAFE?

Box A: Sapphires   **Box B: Rubies**   **Box C: Diamonds**

£1000   £1000   £1000   £500

£500   £500   £500   £500

Money bands

CHALLENGE QUESTION

The thief has dropped the numbers that helped him or her crack the safe code. The code is made up of **products** that appear in the 12 times table.

Find the products, then write them down in order, starting with the smallest number.

What is the safe code?

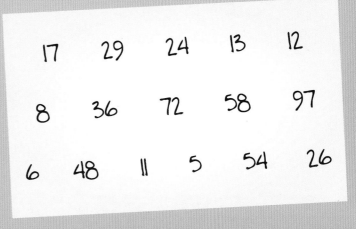

17	29	24	13	12
8	36	72	58	97
6	48	11	5	54	26

(You will find a TIP to help you with this question on page 28)

THE CRIME SCENE

The burglary took place in the mansion's dining room, where the safe is hidden behind a family portrait. This means the dining room is now a crime scene and will be examined by an expert **Scenes of Crime Officer (SOCO)**. The SOCO is in charge of the crime scene and is responsible for protecting the scene and everything in it. SOCOs have the power to stop other people entering a crime scene, even the most senior police officers. SOCOs must be meticulous and pay attention to every detail – they cannot make mistakes. The examination of the crime scene is the most important stage in a criminal investigation. Missing a piece of **evidence** could ruin a case!

SOCO WORK

A SOCO needs to *fix a scene*. This means taking photographs of the crime scene from all angles. The SOCO also makes a sketch of the crime scene to show the positions of doors and windows, and the distances between all the objects in the room.

Look at the photograph of the dining room in the millionaire's mansion. On page 9, you will see four different sketches of the dining room.

Can you work out which of the sketch plans is a correct "picture" of the dining room?

(You will find a TIP to help you with this question on page 28)

EXAMINING A CRIME SCENE FACTS

- First the SOCO checks the scene cordon (the police tape) and adjusts the area of the crime scene if he or she feels it should be bigger or smaller.

- The SOCO then takes photographs and makes sketches. If someone needs to check something about the crime scene at a later date, they can then use these pictures. The photographs will also be used as evidence in court.

- Next, the SOCO searches the scene for evidence. Each item of evidence is given a unique number made up from the SOCO's initials and then a consecutive number; so if SOCO Joe Bloggs has found his third piece of evidence at a scene, it would be numbered JB3.

SOCO FACT

All personnel entering a crime scene must wear protective clothing to stop hairs and fibres from their own clothes **contaminating** the scene. While working at a crime scene, the SOCO wears a one piece paper suit with a hood, a face mask, gloves and overshoes.

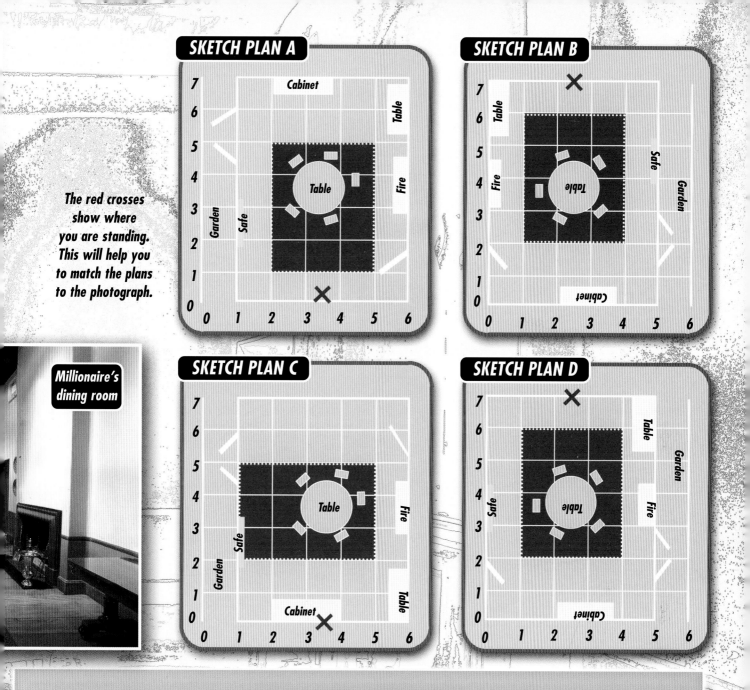

SKETCH PLAN A

SKETCH PLAN B

The red crosses show where you are standing. This will help you to match the plans to the photograph.

Millionaire's dining room

SKETCH PLAN C

SKETCH PLAN D

CHALLENGE QUESTIONS

The SOCO makes a 'crime scene report' listing all the items recovered (found) at the scene. Now you have worked out which sketch plan is a correct picture of the room, you can use the grid on the sketch to find some clues!

Here are some pieces of evidence and their co-ordinates on the grid:

- Muddy footprints (5,2) • Splashes of blood on broken glass (6,2) • **Fingerprints** (3,4) (0,4) (5,5)
- A palm print (2,4) • A single hair (5,4)

a) Which clue is outside the French windows?   b) Which clues are behind the picture in the safe?
c) Where were fingerprints found?   d) Which clues were left just inside the French windows?
e) Where was a palm print found?

(You will find TIPS to help you with these questions on page 28)

EXAMINING THE CRIME SCENE

When searching a crime scene there are two very important areas to examine, the point of entry, or *ingress*, and the point of exit, *egress*. At the mansion you are examining the French windows in the dining room. It looks as though the **perpetrator** used the French windows to come in and out of the house. There are muddy footprints just inside the doors heading into the dining room, and you have found some fragments of glass just outside the doors, where one of the door panes has been broken. You see there are some splashes of blood on the glass. The thief must have smashed the glass and been cut when breaking in!

DETECTIVE WORK

The perpetrator must have escaped through the mansion's gardens, so the police are searching the grounds. Find out how long it would take someone to run between some of the features in the grounds of the mansion.

If it takes about a minute to run 200 metres, how long does it take to run:

1) From the main gate to the mansion?
2) From the main gate to the garage and stable block?
3) From the summerhouse to the boat house via the greenhouse?
4) If the distance from the back gate to the turn off for the boathouse is 300 metres, how long does it take to run from the boathouse to the mansion?
5) How much longer does it take to run from the tennis court to the summerhouse, than the tennis court to the mansion?

(You will find TIPS to help you with these questions on page 28)

THE MILLIONAIRE'S ESTATE

LANDING STAGE

MAIN GATE

LODGE HOUSE

SOCO FACT

If a crime scene is inside a building, the **SOCO** searches from the point of entry to the property, for example, through the garden, towards the main focus of the crime, such as a safe, and then back to the point of exit.

CHALLENGE QUESTION

Here is a diagram of places to visit in the mansion grounds.

How many different routes can you find to visit each of the places once, starting and finishing at the main gate?

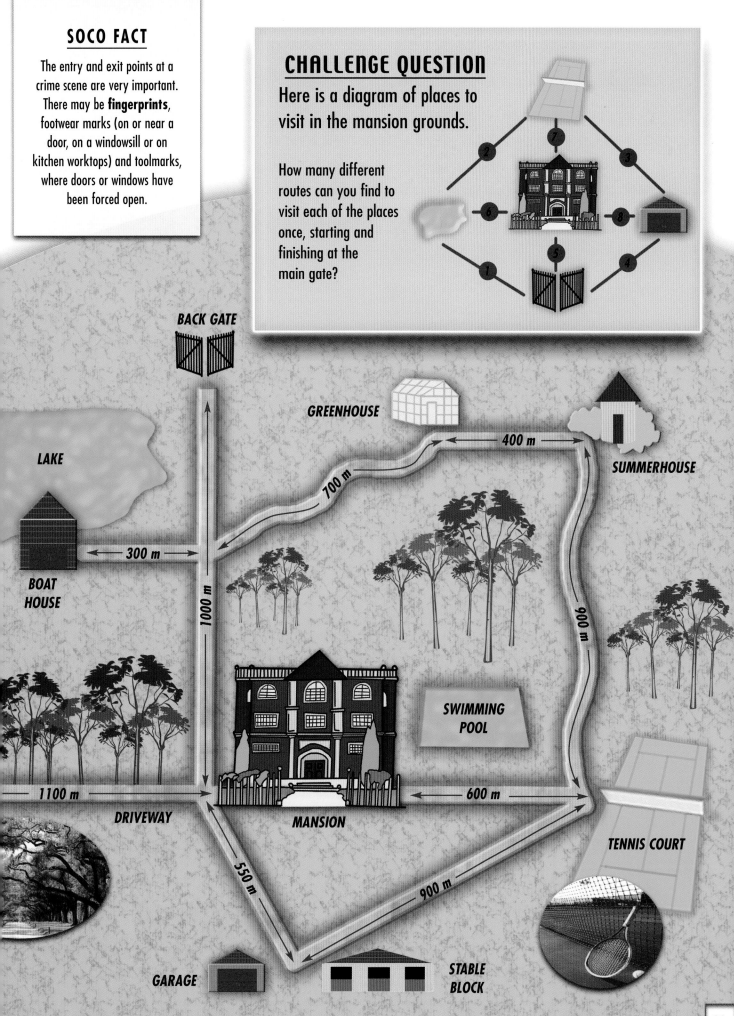

BACK GATE

GREENHOUSE

LAKE

SUMMERHOUSE

400 m

700 m

300 m

1000 m

900 m

BOAT HOUSE

SWIMMING POOL

1100 m

600 m

DRIVEWAY

MANSION

550 m

900 m

TENNIS COURT

GARAGE

STABLE BLOCK

RECOVERING EVIDENCE

The crime scene at the mansion has been sketched and photographed. Now the **SOCO** must find and recover (collect) any forensic **evidence.** Any piece of evidence that is found has to be securely packaged, then labelled with details of where it was found, when and by whom. The most common types of evidence found at crime scenes are blood, hairs, fibres (from clothes), glass fragments, tiny chips or slivers of paint, soil and plant material, footwear and footwear marks, **fingerprints**, items of clothing and documents. When all the forensic evidence is recovered, the SOCO examines the crime scene for fingerprints.

SOCO WORK

You have already shown that you are good at assessing a crime scene.

Now see how good you are at looking for details.
First, study the picture of dining room A. Then look at dining room B.
List all the things that are different in your notebook.

How many differences can you find?

(You will find a TIP to help you with this activity on page 28)

Recovering the blood splashes.

CHALLENGE QUESTION

Fingerprints are usually *latent,* they cannot be seen in normal light. SOCOs use lots of different techniques to find and enhance the prints (make them visible).
The fingerprint can then be photographed or lifted, using clear, sticky tape.

a) Give an **estimate** of the number of fingerprints that you think are on pages 12 and 13. Write your estimate in your notebook.

b) Now count the fingerprints.
How many are there?

(You will find information about ESTIMATING on page 28)

SOCO FACT

SOCOs take *control samples* at a crime scene. For example, if a fingerprint is found, the SOCO will try to find prints (or prints will be taken later) from the people who live at the house. These **elimination prints** will then be compared to the fingerprint found at the crime scene. This helps to show if the fingerprint belongs to the **perpetrator**, or to one of the residents.

SOCO FACT

Close-up photographs are taken of each piece of evidence before it is recovered. Tool and footwear marks are photographed next to a scale (a bit like a ruler), so the photographs can be enlarged back at the lab to life size.

Dining room A

Dining room B

RECOVERING EVIDENCE FACTS

BLOOD

Pools of blood are recovered using a pipette. Blood that has soaked into a surface is allowed to dry and then the material is packaged up. Dry blood is removed using a razor blade or a cotton bud moistened with water.

HAIR

Hairs are normally large enough to see. The SOCO can pick them up using tweezers or lift them using a special sticky tape.

FINGERPRINTS

SOCOs shine special lights on fingerprints, brush them with powders or use chemicals which turn the fingerprint a colour that can be seen. All these methods help the fingerprint show up against its background. Sometimes SOCOs will remove something large such as a front door, and take it back to the lab for enhancement if they believe there could be a fingerprint on it.

GLASS

When pieces of glass are recovered they must be put in plastic containers or boxes. They should not be put in plastic bags, which the glass could cut through, or in glass containers. The glass container could break, mixing with the evidence glass.

WITNESS STATEMENTS

Several good pieces of **evidence** have been found at the crime scene – the footprints, the broken glass with blood splashes, the single hair, the palm print and some **fingerprints**! It is not just physical evidence, such as fingerprints, that are collected at a crime scene. Detectives can also collect verbal (spoken) evidence, by taking **statements** from **witnesses**, **victims** and **suspects**. One of the millionaire's neighbours has given you some interesting information. The neighbour cannot walk very well, so she spends her days watching from her window. On the day of the burglary, she saw someone running from the mansion's back gate dressed in black and wearing a hat!

DETECTIVE WORK

The person the neighbour saw was wearing white trainers and glasses and was taller than the mansion's gate. The gate is – *one hundred and sixty seven centimetres* high.

Everyone who lives or works at the mansion, or who was seen near the house on the day of the burglary, has been interviewed. The suspects were asked if they ever wear glasses, if they own a pair of white trainers and for their height.
Their answers have been put in the DATA BOX.
Use the data to answer these questions:

1) How many people never wear glasses?
2) Who does not own white trainers?
3) Which two suspects are the same height?
4) What is the difference in height between the tallest person and the shortest person?
5) Which of the suspects could the neighbour have seen running from the mansion's back gate?

(Don't forget to write the names of your suspects into your own notebook.)

(You will find a TIP to help you with these questions on page 28)

SOCO FACT

SOCOs are trained in a special interview technique called *cognitive interviewing*. They interview the victims of crimes, then use special 'E-Fit' computer software to produce a likeness of the **perpetrator's** face.

DATA BOX TABLE OF SUSPECTS

SUSPECT	SOMETIMES WEARS GLASSES	OWNS WHITE TRAINERS	HEIGHT
1. Delivery man	Yes	No	1 m 52 cm
2. Millionaire's secretary	Yes	Yes	1 ¾ metres
3. Man seen jogging nearby	No	Yes	2 m
4. The gardener	Yes	Yes	One metre and eighty centimetres
5. The chef	Yes	Yes	174 cm
6. The butler	Yes	Yes	He is not sure, but he is taller than the secretary.
7. The millionaire's maid	Yes	Yes	150 cm
8. Millionaire's personal trainer	Yes	Yes	1 metre 90 centimetres
9. The chauffeur	Yes	Yes	175 centimetres
10. The odd-job man	Yes	Yes	1720 mm

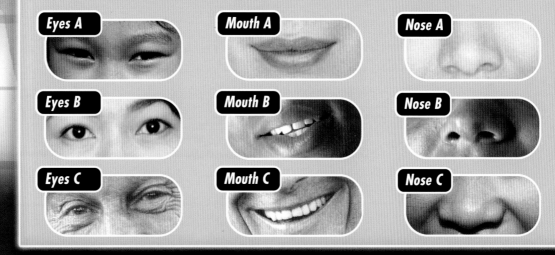

CHALLENGE QUESTION
Below are a selection of 'E-Fit' facial features.
How many different faces can you make using these features?

Eyes A **Mouth A** **Nose A**

Eyes B **Mouth B** **Nose B**

Eyes C **Mouth C** **Nose C**

INTERVIEWING SUSPECTS

The **suspects** have now been narrowed down. There are seven people who could have been the mysterious figure that the neighbour witnessed running from the grounds of the mansion. Do you have the correct seven people written in your notes? The maid has confirmed to you that she discovered the crime. The maid finished dusting in the dining room at 3:40 pm and at that time all was well. When she returned at 4:00 pm with a vase of fresh flowers for the table, the French windows were swinging open and the safe was empty! Now you need to find out what your suspects were doing at the time the crime was committed.

DETECTIVE WORK

On these pages you will see the suspects' **statements**. Each of the suspects were asked what they were doing from 2:00 pm onwards on the day of the burglary.

All the suspects were busy in the afternoon, but some of them had finished their work by 3:40 pm.

Read the statements. Who had time to commit the crime?

SUSPECT STATEMENT: Millionaire's personal trainer

The personal trainer says he was alone in the summerhouse doing yoga for 45 minutes, then he lifted weights for about three quarters of an hour. He started at 2:00 pm.

SUSPECT STATEMENT: The chef

The chef started making bread at 2:00 pm. This was his timetable:

- Set out ingredients and make dough — 10 minutes.
- Make soup while the dough rises — 20 minutes.
- Knock back dough and allow to rise again — 5 minutes.
- Put dough in oven. Tidy up and wait for bread to bake — 35 minutes.

SUSPECT STATEMENT: The secretary

The secretary says she was in her office at the lodge house near the main gate typing letters. She then went out of the main gate to walk to the village to post the letters, but she does not know at what time she left because her watch is broken. It takes 40 minutes to walk to the post office.

SUSPECT STATEMENT:
The gardener

The gardener was busy all afternoon in the greenhouse taking plant cuttings. He started at 2:00 pm and took 8 minutes to plant each cutting. He took 12 cuttings.

SUSPECT INTERVIEW:
Odd-job man

The odd-job man started painting railings by the main gate at 2:00 pm. There are 28 railings and each one took five minutes to paint. (You notice he has painted them all.) The odd-job man says he saw the secretary leave with some letters in her hand as the village clock struck the half hour. He saw the chauffeur drive in the main gate soon after that.

SUSPECT INTERVIEW:
The butler

The butler sat down in the butler's pantry at 2:00 pm and wrote out next week's job rota. For each day this takes 11 minutes.

SUSPECT STATEMENT:
The chauffeur

The chauffeur says she started cleaning the car at 2:00 pm. This took 55 minutes. She then drove into the village to fill up with petrol, she thinks this took about 35 minutes.

CHALLENGE QUESTION

The chauffeur has just remembered the exact time that she returned to the mansion.

She remembers seeing the church clock in her rearview mirror as she drove into the main gate.
What time did the clock say?

(Remember the clock was reversed because it was being seen in a mirror.)

ANALYSING CLUES: THE FOOTPRINTS

The pieces of **evidence** collected at the crime scene have now been given to the **forensic scientists** in the laboratory. It is time to see if we can eliminate some more **suspects**. Footwear prints can be as unique as a **fingerprint.** As we walk about in our shoes each day, we wear them down and they become damaged by small stones or bits of glass. This damage is unique – no other shoe will have the same damage pattern. A footwear mark recovered at a crime scene can be compared with the suspect's shoe to prove that the shoe was at the crime scene. Footwear marks can either be *latent* which means they cannot be seen in normal light or *patent,* they can be seen.

FORENSIC WORK

The footprints found in the dining room at the mansion are patent. No-one was allowed to come in or out of the French windows until the footprints had been photographed and recovered.

The two footprints measured 30 cm and 28 cm in length. Look at the **bar chart** to find out what shoe sizes they are.

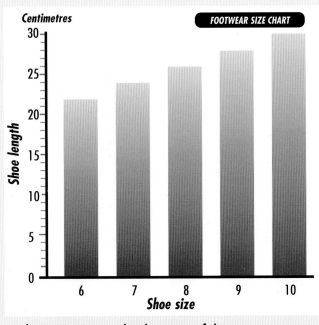

Centimetres

FOOTWEAR SIZE CHART

Shoe length (y-axis) vs *Shoe size* (x-axis: 6, 7, 8, 9, 10)

In the DATA BOX are the shoe sizes of the remaining suspects. Who could have made the footprints?

(You will find TIPS to help you with this activity on page 29)

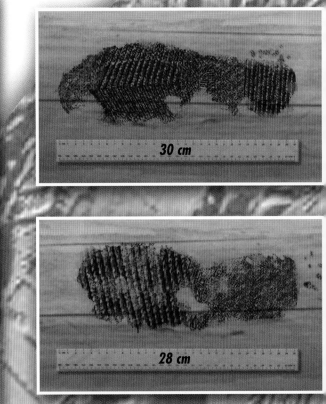

30 cm

28 cm

RECOVERING 3-D FOOTWEAR MARKS

A foot mark left in mud that has dried (a 3-D, or three-dimensional mark) can be cast. A plastic frame (like a little fence) is pushed into the ground around the mark. A casting compound is mixed up and poured into the frame and into the foot mark. When the cast sets, it can be lifted and transported to the laboratory to be examined.

SUSPECTS

SUSPECT	SHOE SIZE
Butler	9
Personal trainer	10
Chef	10
Chauffeur	6
Gardener	9

Examining footwear marks in the lab.

2-D FOOTWEAR MARKS

One way to recover marks left on hard surfaces is to use ESLA (electrostatic lifting apparatus). A special plastic sheet is rolled over the print. An electric current is then passed through the sheet. Any dust particles are attracted to the plastic in the shape of the print. Back at the lab, a powerful light is shone over the sheet, and the prints can be seen and photographed.

Sometimes special paper with adhesive or gelatin is used — like large sticky labels. The paper is placed over the mark. After a few minutes, it is lifted and the dust or mud is transferred to the paper in the same size as the original foot mark.

CHALLENGE QUESTIONS

When you buy a pair of shoes or trainers they have a manufactured sole pattern. These patterns are stored in a computer database. Forensic scientists can use this information to **estimate** the make and model of a shoe.

Study these muddy footprints. The mud on the trainers fills a **fraction** of the markings on each sole.
a) What fraction of the marking is filled in on each of the four shoes?
b) Convert the answers for shoes B and D to **decimal fractions**.

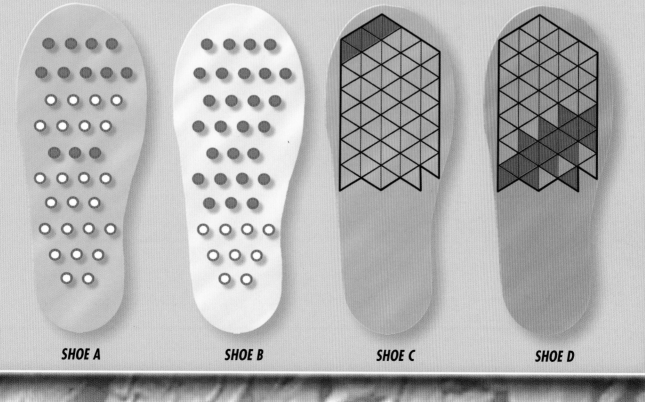

SHOE A   SHOE B   SHOE C   SHOE D

ANALYSING CLUES: BLOOD AND HAIR

We are now analysing the single hair and the blood splashes that were found at the crime scene. The blood has been removed from the glass and is being tested to find out if it is blood type A, B, AB or O. All humans are one of these four blood types. The hair has been mounted on a microscope slide and is being examined at 100 times normal magnification. **Forensic scientists** can then tell whether it is a human or animal hair and confirm the colour of the hair. By examining the hair tip, scientists can even see if the hair has been cut recently and whether it was cut by scissors or clippers.

FORENSIC WORK

The blood found at the scene is type B and the hair found in the safe is brown. We can now eliminate some more **suspects** by comparing their hair colour and blood types.

A chart showing the blood and hair information has been drawn up. One person has been put in the chart already. Draw the chart in your notebook and put the other suspects in the correct sections.

Blood type	Hair colour	
	Brown	Not brown
Blood type B		
Not blood type B		

Who could still be the **perpetrator**?

GARDENER:
Brown hair / Blood type: B

CHEF:
Brown hair / Blood type: A

BLOOD FACT

For many years doctors tried to transfuse blood from one person to another. This often failed because the blood went lumpy, killing the patient. In 1901, a scientist called Carl Landsteiner discovered that all blood is not the same. Landsteiner and his colleagues discovered there are four types of blood. A blood transfusion will only work if blood of the right type is given to the patient.

HAIR FACTS

Approximately 100 head hairs fall out of each person every day, so hair is often found at a crime scene. Hairs from the different areas of the human body look different under a microscope.

A hair is made up of three layers: the CUTICLE (the outer covering), the CORTEX (the inner part) and the MEDULLA (a tube in the centre of the cortex). The cuticle is made of colourless scales that overlap, like the tiles on a roof. The shape of the scales can be used to tell human and animal hairs apart. The cortex is important in forensic work because it has pigment granules that give the hair its colour.

Magnified human hair with cut tip.

PERSONAL TRAINER:
Black hair / Blood type: O

BUTLER:
Brown hair / Blood type: B

CHALLENGE QUESTIONS

About two or three weeks after a haircut, hair tips begin to look rounded. The hair found at the crime scene is still square cut — it has been cut recently!

You are visiting the village hairdresser to check whether any of the brown-haired suspects have had a hair cut in the last week. The hairdresser is going to consult her 'tally chart' of customers.

HAIR COLOUR	NUMBER OF CUSTOMERS
BROWN	//// //// ////
BLACK	////
WHITE	//// ///
RED	//
BLOND	//// //

While the hairdresser checks, see if you can answer these questions:

a) How many customers did she have?
b) How many of her customers did not have white hair?
c) Six of the customers have dyed hair.
   What **fraction** is that of the total?

(You will find information about TALLY CHARTS on page 29)

ANALYSING CLUES: FINGERPRINTS

The patterns of ridges that you have on your hands, fingers and thumbs are unique to you. The ridge patterns form before we are born and they stay the same our whole lives, unless they are damaged by burning or bad scarring. There are sweat pores along the length of the ridges, so if a finger comes into contact with a suitable surface, a thin, normally invisible, impression is left in sweat. This is a **fingerprint**. It means a particular person was at a crime scene, but it cannot prove when. Fingerprint officers compare prints found at a crime scene with inked fingerprints taken from **suspects**, the **victim** and other people who were at the scene.

FORENSIC WORK

If fingerprints match up, the identification is regarded as being *absolute* – the person was definitely at the scene.

Look at these part fingerprints found in the safe at the millionaire's mansion.

1) Which of the **elimination prints** do they match?

a)

b)

c)

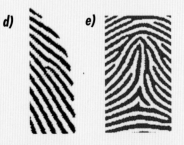
d)   *e)*

ELIMINATION PRINTS

Millionaire

Butler

Gardener

2) Who is now your main suspect?

Suspects are fingerprinted at a police station by a fingerprint officer.

THERE ARE THREE MAIN CLASSES OF FINGERPRINTS:

ARCHES

Ridges enter from one side and exit from the other. Arches can be sub-divided into plain arches and tented arches.

PLAIN ARCH   **TENTED ARCH**

WHORLS

A spiral whorl contains at least one ridge that makes a complete 360° turn around the print.

SPIRAL WHORL

LOOPS

Loops generally have at least one ridge that starts on one side, extends across the finger and curves back to the same side.

PLAIN LOOP

Galton's details

As well as working out what class a fingerprint is, there are tiny details on fingerprints known as *Galton's details*. These can all be useful when comparing fingerprints.

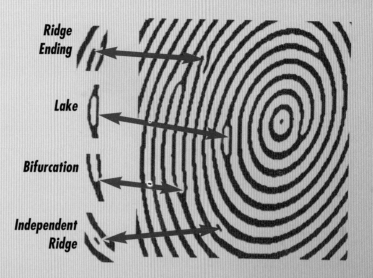

Ridge Ending

Lake

Bifurcation

Independent Ridge

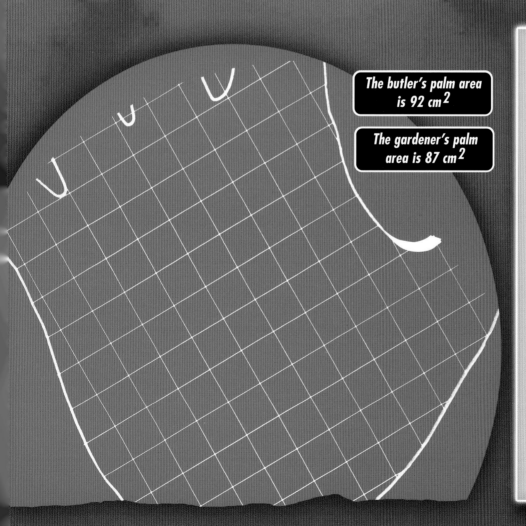

The butler's palm area is 92 cm^2

The gardener's palm area is 87 cm^2

CHALLENGE QUESTIONS

Count the whole squares in this palm print found in the dining room.

Each whole square is one square centimetre, so you can find the area of the palm print in square centimetres (cm^2).

a) Who does the palm print belong to?
b) Who is now your main suspect? (Write it down!)
c) Find the area of the palm of your hand. What is the difference between your palm area and the gardener's? The butler's?

TIME TO CONFRONT YOUR SUSPECT

The investigation is over – who is your main **suspect**? All the **evidence** is pointing towards just one person – the gardener! He had enough time to commit the crime. It could be his footprint in the dining room, his blood on the broken glass and his hair in the safe. The **fingerprints** found in the safe were definitely the gardener's. You receive a telephone call. The village hairdresser has just confirmed that the gardener had his hair cut last week! It is time to confront your main suspect. You find the gardener in the greenhouse, but he is acting suspiciously and refuses to answer any more questions. You decide to arrest the gardener and take a look around.

DETECTIVE WORK

Before he was arrested the gardener was busy sticking together a note. It looks like some sort of code.

Cracking codes is a specialist skill, but in the DATA BOX you will see a grid which will help you to untangle the gardener's secret message.

To use the grid you have to write the number of a row then the number of a column to make a letter.
For example, 15 is *row 1* and *column 5* which gives the letter **e**.
The letter made by 43 is **r**, and 51 is either **u** or **v**.
Use the grid to crack the code.
What does the gardener's secret message say?

The gardener is arrested.

EVIDENCE FACT

Each piece of evidence gathered in a case must have a *chain of evidence*. This is an unbroken chain of written evidence that tells the story of what has happened to the article, from the moment it was recovered at the crime scene, until it appears in court. Every police officer or scientist who comes into contact with the evidence must keep the chain going. If there are any gaps in the chain, the piece of evidence could be considered unsafe to use in court!

FORENSICS FACT

Small amounts, or traces, of evidence found at a crime scene help investigators show that there is a link between the crime scene and a suspect. For example, if we can find the gardener's trainers, we can compare them with the footwear mark found at the scene. Our foot mark contains unique details from the sole of the shoe. These unique damage marks can prove that the gardener's shoe was at the scene of the crime.

DATA BOX CODE CRACKER

	1	2	3	4	5
1	a	b	c	d	e
2	f	g	h	i	j
3	k	l	m	n	o
4	p	q	r	s	t
5	uv	w	x	y	z

2235   4535   452315   45431515

4435514523   3521   452315

22431515342335514415

113414   3435434523 - 52154445

3521   452315   451534342444

1335514345   113414   32353531

2434   452315   23353215

2434   452315   4543513431

CHALLENGE QUESTION

Try making up your own secret code. You can give
each letter a number from 1 to 26, but start with
the first letter of your name as number '1'.

(You will find some more information about making up SECRET NUMBER CODES on page 29)

FINDING THE STOLEN GOODS

The **evidence** found by the **SOCO**, the analysis of the evidence by the **forensic scientists** and the interviews conducted with the **witnesses** and **suspects** have all paid off. The chief suspect, the gardener, has finally confessed. There is just one small problem. The gardener has hidden the money and jewels so that an **accomplice** can pick them up for him if he is arrested. You will need to find the stolen goods and return them to the millionaire before you can close the case. Then you will have to find out who the gardener's accomplice is — but that's another case entirely!

DETECTIVE WORK

You are standing at the tree with the hole in the trunk. Inside, you have found a note for the gardener's accomplice. It gives directions to where the money and jewels are buried.

MAP OF THE GARDEN

Statue

BENCH

SHRUBBERY

FLOWER-BED

WOODLAND

SHRUBBERY

WOODLAND

VEGETABLE GARDEN

BENCH

HERB GARDEN

ROSE GARDEN

Statue

Statue

POND

You are here (starting point)

Using the map of the gardens and the compass, follow the instructions on the note.

Where in the garden are the stolen goods buried?

WHERE TO DIG:

Compass: N, NW, NE, W, E, SW, SE, S

- Go 3 squares north
- 6 squares east
- Diagonally 2 squares south-east
- 2 squares east
- 7 squares north
- 6 squares west
- 1 square south
- Diagonally 2 squares south-west
- 2 squares west
- 3 squares north and dig here!

(You will find a TIP to help you with this activity on page 29)

FORENSICS FACTS

All living things are made from cells. Inside most cells are instructions for making that person, animal or plant, stored as a substance called DNA (Deoxyribonucleic acid). Forensic scientists can test saliva (spit), skin, hair (if there is some hair root present) and blood, and match the DNA to a suspect. A forensic scientist could find DNA in just a single skin cell. This means that just by touching something such as a doorknob, you are potentially leaving behind your DNA. The blood and hair found at our crime scene could be *DNA tested* to match it to the gardener.

CHALLENGE QUESTION

The money and jewels are all buried exactly where the note said. Now they can be returned to the millionaire.

If some of the jewels were cut in half, this is what they would look like. What shapes would they make if you reflected them in a mirror?

a)

b)

c)

d)

TIPS FOR MATHS SUCCESS

PAGES 6–7

DETECTIVE WORK

TIP: Multiplication is the same as doing repeated addition. *For example, 5 × 3 is the same as 5 + 5 + 5.*

Recognising 2-D shapes:

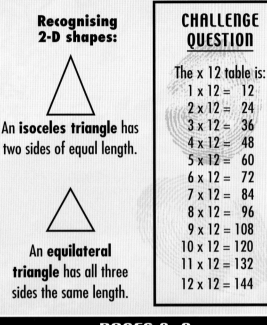

An **isoceles triangle** has two sides of equal length.

An **equilateral triangle** has all three sides the same length.

CHALLENGE QUESTION

The x 12 table is:

1 x 12 = 12
2 x 12 = 24
3 x 12 = 36
4 x 12 = 48
5 x 12 = 60
6 x 12 = 72
7 x 12 = 84
8 x 12 = 96
9 x 12 = 108
10 x 12 = 120
11 x 12 = 132
12 x 12 = 144

PAGES 8–9

SOCO WORK

TIP: Look carefully at the walls. Where is the door and the French windows? Where are the different items of furniture?

CHALLENGE QUESTIONS

Using co-ordinates:

To find the co-ordinates of a point on a grid, you read along the bottom of the grid first, then up the side of the grid.

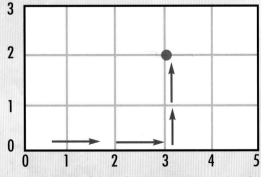

For example, a grid reference of **(3,2)** means **3 steps** along the bottom then **2 steps** up to find the exact point.

PAGES 10–11

DETECTIVE WORK

TIPS:
- If it takes 1 minute to run 200 metres, then it will take twice as long to run 400 metres — that is 2 minutes.
- There are 60 seconds in a minute.

PAGES 12–13

SOCO WORK

TIP: Get yourself organised! Work through this challenge by looking at each part of the picture in turn.

CHALLENGE QUESTION

TIP: An **estimate** is not a guess, but is an answer that we know may be close to what is exactly correct. Being good at estimating helps you to check your maths work.

PAGES 14–15

DETECTIVE WORK

Using units of measurement:

TIP: When you are given measurements in mixed units, it can be helpful to convert them all to the same unit so that they can be compared.

For example, 174 cm and 2 m can be compared as 1.74 m and 2 m, or as 174 cm and 200 cm.

(To help with your conversions see UNITS OF MEASUREMENT on page 29)

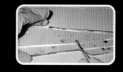

PAGES 18–19

FORENSIC WORK

Interpreting a bar chart:

Bar charts have bars that should always be the same width. It is the heights of the bars that allow you to compare things. In a bar chart you need to know what each bar stands for and what the scale is.

For example, is the scale going up in 1s, 2s, 5s, 10s, 100s, 1000s or some other amount?

PAGES 20–21

CHALLENGE QUESTIONS

Using data in a tally chart:

A *tally chart* is a quick way of recording and counting the number or amount of something. One vertical line (I) is marked for '1', two vertical lines (II) show 2 and so on. The fifth line is then drawn across the first four (IIII). Use your knowledge of the **products** of the x5 table to quickly add when using *tally marks*.

PAGES 24–25

CHALLENGE QUESTION

You can create your own secret code by giving each letter in the alphabet a number. To make the code hard to crack, you can use the first letter of your name as the number '1' (instead of A) and then continue from there. For example, if your name was George or Grace, your code would look like this:

1	2	3	4	5	6	7
G	H	I	J	K	L	M
8	9	10	11	12	13	14
N	O	P	Q	R	S	T
15	16	17	18	19	20	21
U	V	W	X	Y	Z	A
22	23	24	25	26		
B	C	D	E	F		

PAGES 26–27

DETECTIVE WORK

TIP: The line across a square from one corner to the opposite corner is called the diagonal.

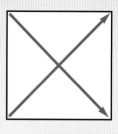

UNITS OF MEASUREMENT

We use two systems of measurement in the UK: *metric* (centimetres, metres, kilometres, grams, kilograms) and *imperial* (inches, feet, miles, ounces, pounds).

METRIC		IMPERIAL	
Length		**Length**	
1 millimetre (mm)		1 inch (in)	
1 centimetre (cm)	= 10 mm	1 foot (ft)	= 12 in
1 metre (m)	= 100 cm	1 yard (yd)	= 3 ft
1 kilometre (km)	= 1000 m	1 mile	= 1760 yd
Weight		**Weight**	
1 gram (g)		1 ounce (oz)	
1 kilogram (kg)	= 1000 g	1 pound (lb)	= 16 oz
Capacity		**Capacity**	
1 millilitre (ml)		1 fluid ounce (fl oz)	
1 litre (l) = 1000 ml		1 UK pint (pt)	= 20 fl oz

Comparing metric and imperial measurements:

1 kilometre = 0.62 of a mile
1 kilogram = 2.2 pounds
0.57 litre = 1 UK pint

ANSWERS ANSWERS ANSWERS

PAGES 6–7

DETECTIVE WORK

1) £5500 was stolen.
2) a) The **equilateral triangle** is in box B.
   b) The **isoceles triangle** is in box A.
   c) The **hexagon** is in box B.
   d) The **octagon** is in box C.
3) A) £595 of sapphires were stolen (7 x £85)
   B) £585 of rubies were stolen (9 x £65)
   C) £800 of diamonds were stolen (8 x £100)

CHALLENGE QUESTION

The code to crack the safe is **12, 24, 36, 48, 72**

PAGES 8–9

SOCO WORK

Sketch plan B is a correct picture of the room.

CHALLENGE QUESTIONS

a) The broken glass is outside the French windows.
b) A single hair and fingerprints are in the safe.
c) Fingerprints were found on the table, on the fireplace and in the safe.
d) Muddy footprints were left just inside the French windows.
e) A palm print was found on the table.

PAGES 10–11

DETECTIVE WORK

1) Five and a half minutes (5 minutes 30 seconds)
2) Eight and a quarter minutes (8 minutes 15 seconds)
3) Seven minutes
4) Five minutes
5) One and a half minutes (1 minute 30 seconds) longer

CHALLENGE QUESTION

Here are the routes you can take:

1,6,7,3,4	4,8,7,2,1	4,3,2,6,5
4,3,7,6,1	5,8,3,2,1	5,6,2,3,4
1,2,7,8,4	1,2,3,8,5	

PAGES 12–13

SOCO WORK

There are 10 differences between the two pictures. Dining room B is different to dining room A because:

1. There is a painting next to the cabinet.
2. There is a painting over the fireplace.
3. The light switch by the door is missing.
4. The rug is smaller.
5. A carving on the top of the cabinet is missing.
6. The painting hiding the safe is straight.
7. French windows have been replaced by normal windows.
8. The chandelier (light) is missing.
9. There is a dog in the room!
10. The bowl of flowers on the table is missing.

CHALLENGE QUESTION

b) There are 26 fingerprints hidden on pages 12 and 13. How close was your **estimate**?

PAGES 14–15

DETECTIVE WORK

1) One person never wears glasses — the jogger.
2) The delivery man does not own white trainers.
3) The secretary and the chauffeur are the same height.
4) Tallest person is the jogger at 2 m and the shortest person is the maid at 150 cm. The difference is 50 cm.
5) The **suspects** are: the secretary, the gardener, the chef, the butler, the millionaire's personal trainer, the chauffeur, the odd-job man.

CHALLENGE QUESTION

Here are the nine different faces that you could make with eyes A.

	MOUTH	NOSE
EYES A	A	A
	A	B
	A	C
	B	A
	B	B
	B	C
	C	A
	C	B
	C	C

The same number can be made with eyes B or eyes C, so the total possible number of different faces is 27.

ANSWERS ANSWERS ANSWERS

DETECTIVE WORK

The following people had time to commit the crime between 3:40 pm and 4:00 pm:

- *The personal trainer* – he finished his yoga and weightlifting at 3:30 pm.
- *The chef* – he finished baking at 3:10 pm.
- *The gardener* – he finished the cuttings at 3:36 pm.
- *The butler* – he finished the job rotas at 3:17 pm.
- *The chauffeur* – she thinks she returned from the village at about 3:30 pm.

The following people did not have time to commit the crime:

- *The secretary* – the odd-job man saw her go off to the village at 3:30 pm, and it takes 1 hour 20 minutes to walk to the post office and back. The secretary was busy until 4:50 pm.
- *The odd-job man* – all the railings are painted, so he must have been painting until 4:20 pm.

CHALLENGE QUESTION

The chauffeur has remembered that on returning to the mansion she saw the clock at 3:40 pm.

FORENSIC WORK

The butler and the gardener (size 9/28 cm) and the trainer and the chef (size 10/30 cm) could have made the footprints.

CHALLENGE QUESTIONS

a) Shoe A: $^{12}/_{36} = ^1/_3$ Shoe B: $^{27}/_{36} = ^3/_4$

Shoe C: $^5/_{60} = ^1/_{12}$ Shoe D: $^{18}/_{60} = ^3/_{10}$

b) Shoe B: $^3/_4 = 0.75$ Shoe D: $^3/_{10} = 0.3$

FORENSIC WORK

The gardener and the butler could still be the **perpetrator**.

Blood type	Hair colour	
	Brown	**Not brown**
Blood type B	🧑🧑	
Not blood type B	🧑	🧑

CHALLENGE QUESTIONS

a) 36 customers b) 28 customers did not have white hair.

c) $^1/_6$ of the total

FORENSIC WORK

1)   a) Gardener   b) Gardener   c) Millionaire
     d) Gardener   e) Millionaire

2) Your main **suspect** should be the gardener!

CHALLENGE QUESTIONS

a) The palm print belongs to the gardener.

b) The gardener should be your main suspect.

DETECTIVE WORK

The message reads: GO TO THE TREE SOUTH OF THE GREENHOUSE AND NORTH-WEST OF THE TENNIS COURT AND LOOK IN THE HOLE IN THE TRUNK.

DETECTIVE WORK

You should be digging in the flower-bed to find the stolen goods.

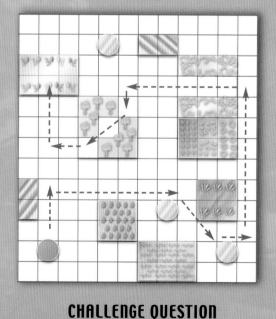

CHALLENGE QUESTION

a) A **regular hexagon** b) A regular **octagon**

c) A rectangle d) An **isoceles triangle**

GLOSSARY

ACCOMPLICE A person who works with or helps another person do something. This word is normally used in connection with people who are committing a crime.

CONTAMINATE When a substance or an item is mixed in with something else. For example, a hair from a police officer mixing with hairs collected as evidence. The evidence would then be contaminated by the police officer's hair.

ELIMINATION PRINTS Fingerprints taken from the victims of crimes or people who live or work at a crime scene. These prints should actually be at the scene and can therefore be eliminated. Any other prints found, have possibly come from a suspect.

EVIDENCE Items found at a crime scene, such as fingerprints, hairs, footwear marks, blood and clothing fibres. Evidence proves a particular person was at a crime scene at some time.

FINGERPRINTS Thin, normally invisible, impressions made in sweat of the ridge patterns on fingers.

FORENSIC SCIENTISTS Scientists who analyse pieces of evidence recovered from crime scenes.

PERPETRATOR A person who commits (perpetrates) a crime.

SCENES OF CRIME OFFICER (SOCO) A specialist investigator who examines the scene of a crime and collects any evidence. SOCOs are civilians, they are not police officers.

STATEMENTS Verbal accounts of something that has happened. Statements are taken from witnesses, victims and suspects by a police officer or other investigator. A statement is then put into writing and becomes part of the evidence for that crime.

SUSPECT A person who the police believe has committed a crime. The person remains a suspect until they are convicted of the crime, or evidence proves they are innocent.

VICTIMS The people that something has happened to, for example, a burglary.

WITNESSES The people who see something happen.

MATHS GLOSSARY

BAR CHART This chart shows information in bars. To read a bar chart you look at the height of the bars against a scale.

DECIMAL FRACTIONS We use a counting system involving tens, multiples of ten and fractions of ten. The decimal point separates whole numbers from decimal fractions. *For example, in the number 672.53, 5 is tenths and 3 is hundredths.*

EQUILATERAL TRIANGLE A triangle with all three sides equal in length.

ESTIMATE To find a number or amount that is close to an exact answer.

FRACTION A fraction is made when a shape or number is cut into equal parts. For example, if a shape is cut into four equal parts, each part is one whole divided by four, or a quarter ($\frac{1}{4}$).

HEXAGON A 2-D (two-dimensional) shape with six angles and six straight sides.

ISOCELES TRIANGLE A triangle with two sides equal in length.

OCTAGON A 2-D (two-dimensional) shape with eight angles and eight straight sides.

PRODUCT The result of multiplying two or more numbers together.

REGULAR Used to describe 2-D shapes that have sides that are equal in length and 3-D shapes with faces all the same shape and size.

t=top, b=bottom, c=centre, l=left, r=right, OFC=outside front cover, OBC=outside back cover

Alamy: OFC, 1, 6, 8-9c, 12, 13, 16br, 19t, 21 background, 22, OBC.